Wake Up Call
The Final Call

Wake Up Call
The Final Call

New and Selected Poems by
Daniel R. Queen

Also featuring poems by
James "Skip" Queen

Queen's Palace Productions
P.O. Box 571
Bladensburg Md 20710
(301) 927-0670

Printed in the United States of America
Library of Congress Catalog Card Number **93-093580**

ISBN : 1-881328-01-5

Contents 5

Wake-Up Call : Final Call

History   14

Political-Poetics   25

Inspiration   37

Just Kickin' It 45

Soulmate 56

Dear Lord 80

Just-Family 87

Nation-Time 94

Food for Thought 108

Admirations 114

The Body Bag Blues 122

Just-Us 136

CR 24/7X9 144

Dedications & Acknowledgments

I would like to dedicate this work of art to the loving memory of my late brother, Robert (Peter) Queen; and to my late lifetime mentor Dr. Dorothy S. Smith. I thank my mother Frances L. Queen, my father Daniel Griffen, my sisters Zina, Anita , Rosa, Mary Jane, and Gloria. My nephews, Frankie and Manzy Queen. To my brother James F. Queen (Skip). Thank you for your earth shaking poems: *Dear Lord, The Original Man, Privates Lines, The Mighty Right, To a Father and a Friend, I love Lovin' you, Thumbs Down to the Beam, Memories, Gun Smoke, Aids,* written by James F. Queen and Timothy C. Plater. Special thanks to my editor, Dr. Virginia B. Guilford (Bowie State University) Deborah Squirewell, Mr. Herman Robinson, Betty Hutton, Edina Walton, Betty Abbott, Michelle Smith, John Raye, Ms. J. A. Minns, Teresa A. Brooks, Grace Seymour, Michelle Roberts, Cathy Hughes, WOL Family, Nation of Islam F.O. I., Rev. Willie F. Wilson U.T.B.C. Family. C.M.P Staff BSU TV. Bill Smith, Vera D. Chesley, Larry Davis, Leslie Farrelle, David Fisher, Jennifer Jackson, Margarate Roderick-Waldenbooks, CR 24/7 x 9: Cress-Welsing Inc.11/11/93. *Wake-Up Call* is a tribute to the Hon. Min Louis Farrakhan, and the Hon. Rev. Willie Wilson U.T.B.C. Tom Baxter for his prints. A great deal of thanks to Protean Gibril of *AGI Images, Inc.* To my mentor and teacher Dr. Frances Cress Welsing, Thanks so very much for helping me to sound, the wake-up call to an up and coming BLACK NATION.

Introduction
Larry Bland

It is not often that a gifted and talented poet of extraordinary insights graces our presence with his reflections of truth. We are fortunate and blessed to be exposed to the rhythmic and dramatics poetry of Daniel R. Queen. His sonnets on racial matters demand that all of us understand the necessity for greater tolerance of a society that is sequestered in a sea of moral and social indifferences. While others banter racism, Mr. Queen orchestrates a magnificent book of oratorical writing, that glorify the emotions and sensitivities of Black America's increasing struggle against the carnages of radical and economic injustices. While white America struggles to build industries to survive, Black Americans struggle against oppression to exist. His selections of subjects and his tribute to African American leadership symbolize his commitment to truth and the need for all Americans to hear this poet's clarion call for equal justice for all of the children of God.

Foreword
J.A. Mimms

Daniel R. Queen's WAKE-UP CALL: The Final Call could be called a "protest piece". But that would be a lame cop-out. Rather, with WAKE-UP CALL the reader senses that he and she are hearing the urgent alarm of ancient drums signaling impending doom. For in its opening pages we are given an overpowering image symbolizing how the black race has allowed itself to be appeased and cajoled into passivity, having willingly filled its belly and mind with deceptions and lies that have kept us weakened and satisfied with our little niche in the world.

And if that image doesn't stir you, Queen's clever phrasing and startling honest language will. In selection like *"We Gotta get Up"* where Queen's pen captures the spirit of Marcus Garvey's call to the black masses, and *"Stolen Legacy"*, in which Queen's words reach out to slap the reader back to consciousness, WAKE-UP CALL pulls no pushes. Queen's pungent lyricism in *"Sleepin' Wit the Slave Master"*, *"Rotten to the Core"*, *"White-Hand in White Glove"*, *"Can't We All Get Along"*, and *"White Supremacy"*, just to name a few, is designed to deflate bourgeoise thinking and bring the reader out of his and her somnolence. Even Queen's tributes to notable black artists aren't window dressing; instead, the reader is made to appreciate the innate talents our race owns outright. Neither should the reader let WAKE-UP CALL's "love poems" in the section entitled *Soulmate* fool him or her either. Queen again heralds and underscores his message of black self-love and respect. What I especially appreciate here is his tender yet striking glorification of the special love that can be had only between a black man and woman.

As you read WAKE-UP CALL, you'll find yourself smiling, frowning, and experiencing a wide range of emotions, as did I. But, make no mistake about it--WAKE-UP CALL: The Final Call accomplishes its mission. It is a book that should be read and digested by every black person in America and the world. But I'll warn you now before you turn this page that you're gonna be shocked by its blatancy. You'll be stung by its honesty. And you most surely will have some of your sensibilities offended. But isn't that what a slap in the face is supposed to do?

11

Wake-Up Call : The Final Call

The Awakening
Wake-Up Call

Wake-Up to the Truth
And Simply uncheck your mind
Those who heed the Final Call
Are those that know the time.

His-STORY

WE GOTTA GET UP
A Tribute to Marcus Mosiah Garvey

When we believe
In a dream come true,
That's a scaffold to the sky
For what we as people can do.

If we stand up for ourselves
And build a mountain of trust,
We can lean on our own helping hands
To do what we must.

Let's make up our minds
That enough is enough
'Cause now is the time
And we gotta get up...

"Up You Mighty People,"
"Ain't We Got No Pride"?
We gotta get up
Our destiny cannot be denied.
"Ain't We Got No Pride"?
Don't you know we gotta get up.

With a sense of purpose
And self-esteem from the heart
There'll be no bad-blood between us
To Keep us apart.

There's nothing a positive sense
Of self can not do,
When you know who you are
And where you are going to.

The Stolen Legacy
A Tribute to Dr. George G.M. James

It just makes me
so down-hearted and sad
when I think about
what you and yours
have done to me and mine
and what we had

For Afrika is the Blood-Root
of Man, and mankind's Family Tree
So the Greeks could not have been
The authors of Greek philosophy.

And Egypt is a semi-precious
Rosette-stone, Stolen But
never to be released
that's why they took Egypt
out of mother-Afrika and put it
in the middle east.
A wicked-white lie
cannot forever stand
the test of time
for the justice of truth
will always free the soul
and uncloud the mind.

Our stolen legacy
is simply the loss
of our sense of self,
After being programmed
for more than four hundred years
to be like somebody else.

Mother-Afrika under
Roman and Greek Rule
was no longer the land of the
Egyptian mystery schools.

And it just makes me
so down-hearted and sad
when I finally realize
What you and yours
have done to me and mine
and what we had.

The Original Man

Part 1

Shackleled and packed
in cargo ships
Never to return
from a one way trip.

Leaving behind
both family and friends
bringing life as they had known it
to a tragic end.

Off to Amerika
Land of the free
but free in America
they would never be.

Unable to move
Chained hand and hand
Thus began the living hell
of the Original Man.

After weeks at sea
they would finally dock.
Then herded like cattle
to the auction block.

Stripped of their names
Stripped of their pride
Humiliated by crowds
who came only to buy.

Not one friendly face
in a strange, strange land
The new beast of burden
became The Original Man.

Work and work
'til it was too dark to see
and told this was the way
God intended it to be.

Divide and conquer
This was the scheme

and degraded in the name
By this all Amerikan dream.

Tortured into submission
then taught self-hate
And to all who did not submit
Death was their fate.
Not allowed to read or write,
Still the old were able to understand
This was not forever to be the life
of the Original Man.

Part II

Then came the war
between the North and the South
and this is what that war
was all about.

The South wanted slaves
physically chained
The North wanted an invisible
chain on their brain.
When the fighting was over
and the prize was won
a new war for the Original Man
had just begun.

Disheartened by the fact
of a promise deferred
All becuz Jim-Crowism
became the new pass-word.

No voice in government
it was time to make a stand
To move forward in the name
of the Original Man.

These were strong people
who survived on their wit
and were glad to take
any job they could get.

Giving services
for only pennies a day
Enduring racial abuse
with little or nothing to say .

Abuse was also physical
Many good people were killed
just so some of the deranged
could get their thrills.

White only, Black only
or so the signs stated,
and many people would die
before the signs were outdated.

Then came Rosa Parks
who is still remembered today
as the lady who refused
And a movement was underway.

A new cry was heard
throughout the land
It was the united voice
of the Original Man.

Yes, Martin was there
to lend a hand,
While Malcolm in his own way
made his stand.

But to all the un-named of the movement
is what this is all about.
Whose loyalty and devotion
left no doubt.

The time had come
for the world to understand
That justice and truth
was the only way
For the original man.

Sleepin' Wit The Slave Master

I can't afford to live,
Let live, and let folks be
'Cause after all is said and done,
Black folk still ain't free.

Some say love comes in all
Colors because love is blind,
But I don't want nothin' to do with
No love across the color line.

To sleep with your enslaver
Is self-hate in the first degree,
'Cause if you sleep wit the slave
Master, you sleep wit the enemy.

Mixed matched soul-mates
For some is a dream come true,
But some things in life you simply
Never get used to.

So let there be no inter-ethnic
lust or love in our very midst,
Until white-supremacy-racism
On planet earth no longer exists.

For all non-white victims
Of the powers that be
The so-called best of both
Worlds in a non-reality.

Everytime I see this mixed-matched madness
That's supposedly color blind,
My past crosses my future and
Cold chills run up and down my spine.

Our sense of self-esteem
And self-love is way out of whack
When we still think mixed-kids
Are pretty, compared to crystal black.

Too many blacks minds
Are still on the plantation
Sleeping with the slave
masters of miscegenation.

True love, they say is all right wherever
You find it, but I say it's all wrong
'Cause we been lookin' forward and
Thinkin' backward much too long.

There can be no justice
There can be no peace
When sleepin' with the enemy
in the belly of the beast.

To sleep with your enslavers
Is self-hate in the first degree,
'Cause if you sleep with the slave
Master, you sleep wit the enemy.

Homeland of The Soul

In the Afrikan
Egyptian Temples of old,
The Body-House of man
was the tomb of the Soul.

The House Negro

To Whom it may concern:
This is a word of wisdom, to the wise
The multicultural, cross-colored-coon
is a House-nigger in disguise.

The Buffalo Soldier
An Ode To the 9 th & 10 th
Cavalries

The True Truth, of Triumph
and Tragedy will forever unfold
as long as the unsung Black Heroes
of the old west is yet untold.

And though his Just-Due
is still yet undone,
there's a Buffalo warrior
in every child of the sun.

To unhonor and dishonor
An officer and gentleman
was the law of the land,
and somewhere lost in the pages
of his-story is the true-truth
and Glory of the Blackman.

Denied and Pushed aside,
Buffalo Soldiers are
the super-soul troopers
who fought bled and died
to protect the keepers
of the pilgrim's pride.

Buffalo troopers were by far
The best that could ever be
But there's no home, for the brave
in the homeland of the free
for America's unsung Black warriors
of the 9th and 10th Cavalries.

White-Hand in White Glove

I pledge Allegiance
To the flag of the united
Snakes of Amerika
and to the Republic of White-Folk,
For White-Folk, For which it stands
One nation under a Blu-eyed Devil
With liberty and Just-us
For All, White-Folk....Only.

Political-Poetics

Slick-Willie In The White House

The political-propaganda
of slick-willy and goofy gore
will surely keep the grass-root
homeless and the workin' class poor.

Some say our savior
has arrived, but to me
He ain't done a thang
Cuz the powers that be
Control slick-willy like a
puppet on a string.

So whether Donkey
or Elephant by name,
The two party system in Amerika
is still one in the same.

And I refuse to go on
lettin' all come what may
and be quiet as a mouse
gonna keep way-out willy's
Feet to the fire, as long as
he's the man in the white house.

With no place to call home
and no chicken in the pot,
All the hand shakin; baby kissin'
Smiles Don't mean an offa lot
to a half-hungry family
Who simply have not.

In your picture perfect
Public persona, they tell me
You can make a tenor-sax talk
And I know what they're sayin'
But I can't dance to
The music you're playin'.

It's the same old blu-print
For more talk, of hard times
And social economics blues

But when it comes to justice,
Jobs, and Taxes, everybody don't
Pay the same amount of dues.

Yet the political propaganda
of Slick-Willy and Goofy-Gore
Will surely keep the grass root
Homeless and the workin' class poor.

And I refuse to go on
Lettin' all come what may
And be quiet as a mouse
Cuz we gotta keep Slick-Willy's
Feet to the fire, as long as
He's the man in the White House.

Stand Up For Statehood

It's time to get real
with the capitol city
king bees on capitol hill,
so here's the new deal.

Let the new world order start
in the capitol city of the nation
cause I'm fed up with the feds
on this federal city plantation.

D.C. is the last
colony in the nation
Where we the people can't vote
for our own representation.

If you wanna free D.C.
for the common goal
of the common good,
stand up for D.C. statehood.

Our time has come
and it's our moral obligation
to make D.C. the first black
state in the nation.

The opponents of D.C. statehood
are all the way strong,
but for goodness sake give
yourself the right to be wrong.

For the common goal
of the common good
Why not take a stand
for D.C. statehood.

For the love of your people
and the unjust laws of the land
give yourself the right to
stand up and take a stand.

Time to stop crawlin' to congress
with our feet in our hand;
"We gotta plan our work

And work our plan."
It's time to take a stand.
Ain't no time to be consoled.
Non-Representation
With High-Taxation
Has taken its toll
The federal taskmaster
Is still in control.

Capitol-city statehood
Is an up hill battle
Every step of the way
And whether right or wrong
Some folk simply say
It's too black and too strong.

But to make D.C.
All that it can be
For the common good
What we need is D.C. statehood.

The spirit of unconditional
Home rule will only be free
When New Columbia is a
Full fledge reality.

And for the common concern
Of the common good,
Our time has come
And it's our moral obligation
To make D.C. the fifty-first
State in the Nation.

Private Lines

They have given themselves the right
To bug everyone's phone
And the constitution is on ice
In parts unknown.

They tell us it's to stop conspiracy
And similar shady deals
I say Hoover was a mother
With Webster hot on his heels.

There was a time when private lines
Were something we paid for and usually got.
Well, they left us with the lines;
It's just the privacy we have not.

They say it's for crime prevention
Or in the interest of national security,
But if they were taking care of the nation right,
Our homes would be left to you and me.

We've been told this type of thing
Only happens under a dictator's rule
Well, it sure looks like our leader
And the tyrannical rulers
Went to the same damn schools.

So when in your home
You use your phone
For business, or just to call a friend,
Have no fear, But don't talk too clear
The FBI might be listening in.

Public Enemy No One
A Poem For P.E.

Count down to Armageddon
it's another Def. Jam
where the enemy strikes Black.
But as a Rebel without a pause
it takes a nation of millions
to hold us back.

It don't take too much
for a brother or sistah to be
too-black and too-strong,
so show 'em what you got
and don't believe the hype
whether right or wrong.

As the prophet of range
and the masters of the art
of war, Brothers gonna work it out
for white-genetic annihilation
and the fear of a black planet
is what it's all about.

The Serpent

If you wanna survive
expect the unexpected
and live to make a better way,
because ain't nothing like
these united-snakes of
Amerika today.

Run-Jesse-Run
For Rev. Jesse Jackson

Run-Jess-Run, Run-Jesse-Run
Keep on keeping on Run-Jesse-Run
You've got to be strong. Run-Jesse-Run;
Keep on pushing on. No more paying dues; put on
Your running shoes, and just Run, Jesse, Run.

The Wages Of War

GREETING!
Have you heard the latest
Of war-time NEWS?
Saddam Hussein is giving
Good-time Charlie the blues.

Some say, Armageddon
Is just around the bend
And if so, could this be
The beginning of the end.

It seems to me
Uncle Sam's in a hell of a fix
And as quiet as it's kept,
Hue-man blood and oil don't mix.

But black blood is thicker than oil,
No matter what the cost,
Cause the wages of war
Only add up to a total loss.

So before we send another soldier
To die in the Persian Gulf,
Let's make a way for Peace
And call the whole thing off.

Some say Armageddon
Is just around the bend.
And if so, could this be
The beginning of the end.

In a world of money, greed
And non-stop material gain,
America is at war for more than
The aggressions of Saddam Hussein.

For there can never be peace
In the so-call middle east
Without the scope, and full score
Of why Mr. Bush is so hell-bent on war.

The wages of social-economic
Justice, at home denied,
Is nothing less than
Justifiable genocide.

So sign on the front line
And be all, you can never be
For the new world order
OF WHITE SUPREMACY.

Can' t We All Get Alone
For Rodney King

As long as
right is still right
wrong is ever wrong
I say hell-no brother Rodney
There Just Ain't no way
we can all get alone.

Can we all get alone?
nigger...please!

So long as America
is the hate-full police state
that it has always been,
The so-called ReBirth
of America as a nation
is gone with the wind.

Can't we all get along?

How can we all get alone?
Keep hope alive and live
The King of love's dream
when the wicked-way of
white-folk is never
all that it seems.

From Martin King
To LA's Rodney King
who's right or who's wrong,
does it really matter?
Cause what I wanna know
is can we all get alone.

As long as
right is still right
wrong is ever wrong,
I say hell-no, Brother Rodney,
There Just Ain't no way
we can all get alone.

Can we all . . . get along? nigger please!

Rotten To The Core

When the naked truth
is a natural, livin' lie,
Racism and White Supremacy
is American as apple pie.

Becuz from the City of Angels
to the Charm City of Baltimore
There's a worm in the Big Apple
That's racist and rotten to the core.

And ain't no such thing
as equal justice in pity,
when your neck's in the noose
of the Big Apple City.

If America was about the business
of practicing all that she preach
There would be no such place
as South Central or Howard Beach.

From Down-South to Up-South
They're all out ta' lunch,
and a few Bad Apples just
might spoil the whole bunch.

Becuz from the City of Angels
to the Charm City of Baltimore,
There's a worm in the Big Apple
That's racist and rotten to the core.

Inspiration

Becuz I'm Special

Becuz I'm special

I love my sense of self
And it's not for sale.
I know who I am,
And I refuse to fail.

The power of I am
Is my mind's master-key
For the way of the will
Is the life-force in you and me.

The sacred-source
Of all life's wealth
Is simply in how
You look at yourself.

...becuz I'm special

I know who I am
I've got the power to succeed.
And in the spirit of faith
I've got all that I need.

A blessing in disguise
As evidence of things not seen
Is the secret of success
In the seed of self-esteem.

Becuz I am, that I am
Ain't no way I can let myself down
Hang ups, and setbacks, are only
steppin' stones to higher ground.

...becuz I am special

I love my sense of self
And it's not for sale.
I know who I am,
And I refuse to fail
Just becuz ... I am special.

Just Do It

If you go for it
And just do it
You'll find that there really
Ain't nothin' to it.

As long as right is right
And wrong is still wrong
Save all second thoughts
No lookin' back from now on.

Just do it
Shoot your best shot'
Ain't nothin' to it
Give it all you got
Just do it.

A moment of truth
Can not be sold or brought
But to a hungry mind
It's a taste of food for thought.

Learn to love yourself
In grand style and grace
Just let yourself go 'cause
Ain't no time to waste.

Just do it ... Just ... Do It.

You can win but don't let
Surface thrills lead you astray
You gotta know your mind, to trust
What your heart has to say.

Speak of faith, work and success
And at once it's on its ways to you,
But keep the faith beloved, its
Been tried, tested and found true.

Just Do It... Just... Do It.

Take it from me
A whole new world
Is at work for you
When you find the key
To the creative source
Of your fate's destiny.

Just Do It. . .
Shoot your best shot
Ain't nothin' to it
Give it all you got

Just Do It. . . .

Do It For The Children

In the love of every man,
Woman, boy and girl
You can find the key
To the heart of the world.

For each and everyone
Gotta find a better way
To do, what some say
Just can't be done.

Do it for the children.
In all that you do and say
Do it for the children
A lifetime of love
Gotta be a better way
Do it for the children.

Teach the children the truth.

The innocence of a child
Is the seed of truth for all to see.
Teach the children the truth; they're
The fruit of the family tree.

There's so much the world needs
That there's just too little of.
But all we've really got to do
Is give a little more love.

Do it for the children.
In all that you do and say
Do it for the children.
A lifetime of love
Gotta be a better way
Do it for the children.

Teach the children the truth.

The School Of Life

From the school of life
I've got a master's degree
in the course of a life time
from the school of life's university.

And just becuz ain't no letters behind
your name, don't make you dumb.
life is a school you graduate into
but never really graduate from.

Cuz just when you thought
you passed the point of no return
There's a train of thought that says
You're never too old ta learn.

For the spirit of truth
will never fail to show
the school of life will teach
you all you need to know.

No matter how long you live n' learn
or where you might look
life will always teach you things
you can't find in a book.

The voice of experience thru
struggle, stress and strife
is a master-mind teacher
standing on the principles of life.

I am a scholar in the school of thought
beyond the test of time.
I am a child of the Universe
A student of life by design.

Listen with the inner-ear
think with the universal mind
for creative vision will give you
insight into the ties that bind.

... And from the school of life
I've got a master's degree
in the course of a life time
from the school of life's university.

More Important

To free your mind
And be all you need
And want to be,
Just remember it's more
Important to read and think
Than to watch TV.

Mind Power

Thru divine-inspiration
It's never too late
To take daily time
To just sit and meditate.

Wake Up and Smell the Coffee

Life is for living
And love is the cream of life's crop.
Wake up and smell the coffee of life
It's good to the very last drop.

For when the love of life
Becomes the taster's choice
'Tis then you hear life's music
And you're in tune with the inner voice.

So if you want to be happy
And you want to be free,
You've got to wake up early in the morning
And smell the coffee.

Once you forgive your heart
For wasting love to hate
Then the sweet smell of life's coffee
Can be your Coffeemate.

Know that trials and tribulations
Are all a part of life's brew
But when your soul is grounded in faith
There's nothing that you can't do.

Know that triumphs and tragedies
Are a part of life too
Yet the faith of even a mustard seed
Will surely see you through.

So if you want to be happy
And you want to be free
You got to wake up early in the morning
And smell the coffee.

Just Kickin' It

Deep and Quiet Love
Tribute to Eddie Kendricks

Can I be your deep and quiet
Love, you cream of the crop?
I'm hooked on your love
And I just can't stop.

When something's burning
Deep in my heart's desire,
There just ain't no smoke
Without fire.

You're the love of my dreams,
My sweet-honey-brown.
You're the melody of my life
And I'm lovin' you the second time around.

When the newness is gone
For you, I'm born again
And forever happy to be
Your intimate friend.

From me to you
Your wish is my command
Maybe I'm a fool to love you
But it's out of my hands.

Because when somethin's a burning
Deep in my heart's desire,
There just ain't no smoke
Without fire.

A Pocket Full Of Miracles
A Tribute to Smokey Robinson
& The Miracles

Singer, Songwriter
Lyricist, Producer and Poet
Smokey is the Shakespeare of Soul
For those who didn't know it.

With a stroke of genius
And a creative spark,
You were the master-miracle
Of Motown's trademark.

As a poet of passion,
You've really got a hold on me.
The way you work wonders with words
Is like pillow-talk poetry.

Your quiet storm of strength
Is felt in each and every line.
Your warm-way with words and women
Puts me in a Motown state of mind.

From a soft sensuous rock
To a groove that makes it funky,
Ain't nothin' like The Miracles
Doin' Mickey's Monkey.

And OOO Baby, Baby
Baby come close.
You know that you know
Just where it's at.
And the way you do, the things
You do, I like it like that.

You are the composer
That touches the inner most me
The only crown-prince of song
in the Motown family.

And as a poet of passion
You've really got a hold on me.
The way you work wonders with words
Is like pillow-talk poetry.

47

The Soul Of Sam Cooke

As the idol of a
Whole soul-generation,
Sam was a lady's man
Of sweet temptation.

With a superior sense of timing
And a vocal style all his own,
Sam had a way with words and music
That was his and his alone.

With so much satin-soul
Straight from the heart,
The man and his music
Just can't be set apart.

In lingering love-notes
Of pure gospel-soul,
Sam could yodel his way
Into the hearts of the young and old.

Whooa-ooh-oh oh oh!

His soul-stirring
Masterful work of art
Could melt ice cubes in an igloo
To win a Woman's heart.

As a prolific songwriter
And artist of master control,
Sam Cooke sang and wrote
From the very heart of his soul.

He was the man who embodied
Soul-music beyond all doubt,
A smooth, sensuous soulmate
Who crossed over but never sold out.

With a superior sense of timing
And a vocal style all his own,
Sam had a way with words and music
That was his and his alone.

Incredible, irreplacable, unforgettable
And no matter where you look
No one can ever replace the
Immortal soul of Sam Cooke.

Whooa-ooh-oh-oh- oh!

Love In The Key Of Life
A Tribute To Stevie Wonder

Love in sweet harmony
Is an all time paradise,
For the music of my mind
Is love in the key of life.

And with each beat of my heart,
I love every little thing about you.
I love having you around cuz
Where I'm comin'from, I see
Visions of higher ground.

So if you really love me,
Hey love, what can I say.
Thru the ebony eyes of your
Finger tips, loves in need of love today.

I was made to love you.
Don't know if it's magic
Or simply somethin' from
Out of the blue,
But nothin's too good for my baby.
I never had a dream come true,
But I just called to say
I love you.

You are the sunshine of my life
And soulfully second to none.
I don't know why I love you,
But I'll blame it on the sun.

Our love light in flight
Is a rhythm in the sky,
And for once in my life
It's simply you and I.

A Motown State Of Mind
For Berry Gordy &
Smokey Robinson

What some dead beat
Detractors once called
Nothin but assembly line soul,
Today have become the true
Essence of pure black gold.

When the magic in the music
Of the Motown sound
Was on top and in full control,
The sound of young America
Was the sound of the Motor City Soul.

The Glory of the Motown story
Makes it one of a kind,
Cuz the music of the Motor City
Puts me in a Motown State of Mind...

And every time I hear
Motown music on my radio,
I can't help but wonder
Just where did our love go.

For the soul of Tamla Motown
Gordy and Hitsville U.S. Of A
Lovin' you is sweeter than ever
And it's got to be that way
Cuz it's so very hard to say
Good-Bye to Yesterday.

Forever, For Always
For Everlastin' Love
I do believe Heaven
Must have sent you from Above.

'Cause in a world of music
Where the further you look
The less you see,
The Magic in the Music
Of the Motor-City
Is All I Need For Me.

If it's what's in the Groove
That counts, no matter what
You're puttin down,
Nothin' can ever
Take the Place of that
Motor City Sound.

When the Magic in the Music
Of the Motown Sound
Was on top and in full control,
The sound of Young America
Was the sound of the Motor-City Soul.

For what some dead beat
Detractors once called
Nothin' but assembly line soul
Today have become the true
Essence of pure black gold.

Honeymoon In Heaven
For Marvin Gaye &
Tammi Terrell

What love has
Joined together
Just for me and you
Was made in paradise.
And for once in my life
This love is true.

You see, ain't nothin'
like the real thing.
What more can I say;
I was born to love you
Forever, and forever
came today.

You're a wonderful one,
Twenty-four seven.
You're my pride and joy,
My honey-moon in heaven.

All it takes is you and I.
For me and you
Ain't no fun bein' in love
Alone, cuz it takes two.

When it comes to
Lovin' and being' loved,
It's not about material things or money,
Cuz I'm a stubborn kinda fellow
And I'm too busy thinkin'
Bout my honey.

And I'll be doggone
It's so peculiar, yet
That's the way love is
And all know it's true
But oh, how sweet it is
to be loved by you.

You're a wonderful one
Twenty-four seven.
You're my pride and joy
My honey moon in heaven.

This old heart of mine
Is weak for you.
You're my natural high,
Can't help but love you
Your unchanging love
Is all I need to get by.

Your precious love
Is always on my mind,
For Lovin' you is a
Dream of a life time.

That's why
What's hard for one
Is easy for two,
Cuz there's a little bit
Of heaven in everything
You say and do.

You're a special
Part of me,
My life long, lady love
My queen honey bee.

You're such a wonderful one,
Twenty four seven.
You're my pride and joy,
My honey moon in heaven.

The Epic Hero
A Tribute to Michael Jackson

Say, Say, Say,
It's your hallelujah Day
Yet you've just begun
But still you're such a lovely one.

You're such a rhythm child
You and Billie Jean, But Don't
Blame it on the boogie' Cause
You're the dancing machine.

With the gift of song
In your heart and soul
The way you move and groove
It's like remote control.

Startin' Somethin'
Is your claim to fame
And if they can't beat it
Who's to blame.

Like no one
I've ever seen or heard
You're an epic hero
In every sense of the word.

Working day and night
And going places can be rough
But don't stop 'til you get
Enough.

When we rock with you
Your body language says it all
'Cause that's the thriller magic
That keeps us dancing right off the wall.

You're such a rhythm child
You and Billie Jean, But don't
Blame it on the boogie 'cause
You're the dancing machine.

Soulmate

Soulmate

When all we have
is the love of one another,
black on black love
is love in livin color,
cuz ain't no love like the love
between a sister and a brother.

Hip-Hop Honey

Don't get caught-up in
The sugar - coded, sweet nothin's
of some hip-hop honey's in the hood
Cuz when you add it all up
your experience in life will help
you subtract the bad from the good.

Love me, for me

Not for what you think I am
and not for what you want me to be,
But if you want my love for life
you gotta love me for me.

The Dog v.s. The Bitch

The black father of the whole human
family ain't nobody's dog
And despite the claim to fame
Of Joe six pack, or the famous and rich,
The black queen mother of all creation
ain't nobody's bitch.

From A lover To A Friend

I guess it's the beginning of the end.
and from a lover to a friend,
maybe one day, we can do it all again-
from a lover to a friend.

Living a Lie for Love

What kinda fool
Do I have to be
To open my own eyes
and make myself see.

Everybody's somebody fool
and all know it's true
so who am I and what am I
To you?

When hurt to your heart
and all you can do is cry,
all that's left is an
unnatural-high.

But stand for truth
and truth will stand for you
If you're 'bout to fall,
Cuz when you gotta live
A lie for love, it can drive
you somewhat off the wall.

So . . . between my head
and my broken heart,
The beginning of the end
Is a brand new start.

Nobody Wants A fool

All the bitter-sweet
Nothin' sensations
Only add up to a
lifetime of infatuation.

A fool is one who can't face
Life standing on his own two feet
Cuz he's much too busy
Taking the bitter with the sweet.

And I tell you
Time and time again
No one wants a fool
For a lover or a friend.

You know all the money
In the world can't buy love
And ain't no exception to the rule
Cuz it's not in human nature
To love and respect
The wisdom of a fool.

Don't let foolish pride
go to your head and blow your cool,
for the moral of the story is you don't
have to be nobody's fool.

Games People Play

Full of nothin'
but emptiness inside
I've learnt how to live
with my foolish pride.

But sometimes the things love
Will make you do and say
won't free your heart from
The games people play.

Play-mates Undercover

You left me hangin'
on an unnatural high.
I was in love alone
and just livin' a lie.

You were my breath of life
my life time friend
but it was only the beginning
of the end.

When you walked out
on me without a sign,
I was so in love with you
I almost lost my mind.

Thought you were
my soul-mate, my endless lover
But we were just
Play-mates undercover.

When all I needed
was a brand new start,
you just up and had
A change of heart.

It's so hard to believe
This could really be
But that's how your love
Changed on me.

You must have been
God's gift to all human-kind
you were my lite-of-day,
my mid-nite sunshine.

And when you walked
Out on me without a sign
I was so in love with you
I almost lost my mind.

Thought you were
my soul-mate, my endless love
But we were just
playmates, undercover.

Declaration of Independence

This is my Declaration of Independence,
And I swear I've reached the point
Where I just don't care for a love
That's been going nowhere.

The foundations of love
We just could'nt find;
We were both lost in time.

We were just strangers in our youth
Seeking self-satisfaction
And over looking the truth.

This is the reality of something old,
Something new, something so sad and blue
A Declaration of Independence
of me from you.

So this is my
Declaration of Independence
From a life built on something
Other than love.

With our hearts
We hold these truths to be self evident
That all in life and love is never fair.
You see, our pursuit of happiness
Was founded on quick sands of sin
And shame, for the cause was created equal
And we have ourselves to blame.

For in all truth
Our united statements of love
Were just words in the wind
Spoken but never felt within.

And we both know there's no sense
In sayin' or even thinkin'
We can make it work
In a matter of time
Because the foundations of love
We couldn't find.
So this is my Declaration of Independence.

Second to None

To give of yourself
Is easier said than done
'Cause heaven only knows
You're second to none.

And for all 'n all
That it's worth,
I'll have my Honeymoon
In heaven, right here on earth.

From your bittersweet beauty
To your split-personality,
Your self-righteous celibacy
Have taken its toll on me.

And from the hand writings
I see on the wall
None from nun
Leaves nothing at all.

"Someone to Come Home To"

I need someone
who can give a little T.L.C.
I want somebody who will
be there just for me.

I'm so very tired
of being lonely and alone.
I need a special someone
I can call my very own.

When things go wrong
and life's wearing a frown
A house is never a home
If there's no love around.

I want a love...for life
That will be ever so true
and all I need is someone
To come home to.

All I want is someone
To have and to hold
Someone to love me
For me soul to soul.

Thoughts and wishes of you
Won't leave me alone
Only your love and devotion
Can give my heart a home.

They say all things in time
But time just won't wait
I need a honey-made in heaven
A special soul-mate.

When things go wrong
and life's wearing a frown
A house is never a home
If there's no love around.

I want a love . . . for life
That will be ever so true
and all I need is someone
To come home to.

Love's Honorable Mention

At times, it seems
We were always worlds apart
from the very start, cause something
Deep within said we'd never be more
Than first class friends
But if love is the key
To your heart's hall of fame
On the honor roll of your soul,
I shall engrave my name
And when warm memories
Of the sunshine we shared
Stand your heart at attention,
Just think of me as love's Honorable mention.

Natural High

On the wings of love
I get high, high naturally
When you're close to me.
And as all things in time
Do unfold, sweet sensations of love
Ignites my heart and soul.
To a natural high on happiness.

Only One You

When I feel I need
my very own inner space,
inside of your love for me
There's a very special place.

The true love of you
is always on the one
you're a simply special
kinda' someone.

There's only one you
That's always on my mind
like never before two hearts
Can be one of a kind.

And just as long as
one and one is two,
I'm gonna live for love
Cuz there's only one you.

...only one you.

The Right To Be Wrong

Wish I could
mend my mistakes
and just start a new
For neither here nor there
will I ever find
another you.

Think of your feeling of love
as a rendezvous with reality
then give yourself the right
to be wrong about me.

Cuz after being cured from
the call of the wild
and livin' a likeable lie,
it's so very hard to say
the simple words
good-bye...

Love's Moody Moods

One minute you feel
like love, can be something like
A vampire bite to the neck
Then in a maze of moody-moods
The after-glow of love
in full effect.

Love's Long Cold Summer

In a maze of endless
mixed emotions and self-doubt,
The heart-burning fires of love
have burned themselves out.

I thought you'd always
be there, you were my lover
my life time friend
and all time just came
to a sudden end.

Livin' thru Hell
to get to Heaven
can be Paradise.
But the Beginning
of the end has become
The coldest of my life.

So from a long and lonely
cold Summer's walk in the park
I caught walkin' pneumonia
From a frost bitten heart.

For deep down
in my sun-stroked soul
even the Summer sun
has suddenly grown cold.

Melting memories
of high hopes and dreams
still linger in my mind
as Love's heat-wave of unhappiness
sends hot-cold chills
up and down my spine.

And from a long and lonely
Cold summer's walk in the park
I caught walkin' pneumonia
from a frost bitten heart.

Becuz after a endless
sad-happy, heartbreak story
all that's left is the pain
of Love's Faded Glory.

Best Wishes

My life was just a darkened place
Then into my life you came
Your sunshine replaced the darkness
Joy replaced my pain

Now you've taken it all away
leaving me alone again
Seems I've been losing at love so long
I don't know how to win

There's just one thing
I'd like to ask before I depart
Never, never let another do to you
What you have done to my heart!

I care too much to wish you anything
But happiness and all the best
You are far too precious
to settle for any less

Just keep in mind what I said
And I'm not saying it to be smart
Never, never let another do to you
What you have done to my heart!

Love took me for a Ride

I keep tellin' myself
One less pain, don't stop no show
But everytime I turn around
I end up somewhere I don't wanna go.

The way you smiled
At me, called my name
And acted real coy
The love I never had
Played with a heart
Like a child would a toy.

Infatuation
Sweet Sensation
Imagination
Sweet Temptation

One touch of your hand
And I was on a natural high.
Couldn't see, what I needed
To see, I livin' a lie.

When it came to
Grace, Charm and style
You had all it took
And when it came to
The hurt of a heartbreak
You wrote the book.

My imagination
Was workin' overtime
Love took me for a ride
And I almost lost my mind.

What I thought
Was a second chance
Only made me a victim
Of circumstance.

And it's so hard to face
The fact, that I've been had
While under the influence
Of a love gone bad.

Infatuation
Sweet sensation
Imagination
Sweet Temptation

The love of my life
Took me for a ride
I tried to play it cool
And keep it locked away inside
But I'm hurt to my heart
By the widsom of my foolish pride.

Between my head
And my heart, I was so
Into somebody else
But after a head on
Collision, with love
I finally found myself.

But love, took
Me for a ride...

Behind close doors
Intimate Strangers

I know you would
Not believe a single word
If the walls behind
Close doors, Could tell you
All that they've
Seen and heard.

Who would had thought
Mr. and Mrs. Do Right had
Somethin' shady goin' on
Who would had thought
Such a perfect combination
Could turn out so wrong.

For this with all
My heart, I truly believe
Any man who beats 'n' abuses
A woman don't deserve to breathe.

Somewhere behind closed doors
On the other side of the wall
Somebody's Fussin' 'n' fightin'
And it don't make no sense at all.

But if the walls behind
Closed doors could talk
I wonder what they'd say
Cause if this is what
They call love, there
Just ain't no way.

After breath takin' screams
And a soul searchin' silence
That chilled me to the core
I dialed 911, cause I just
Could'nt take it any more.

Another sleepless night
And the best of intimate strangers
Are up and at it again
And after the maze of mind games
The only thing left is the
Beginning of the end.

On the outside
Some folk live the
Picture perfect dream
But somehow on the inside
Things ain't at all
What they seem.

Somewhere, between
A lover, a friend
And an intimate fool
Somebody forgot to
Live up to the essence
Of the golden rule.

For this with all
My heart, i truly believe
Any man who beats 'n' abuses
A woman don't deserve to breathe.

Dear Lord

A Prayer

Through some things in life
Are neither here nor there,
I plan to stay a believer
In the power of prayer, for
We all have crosses to
Bear.

Dear Lord

Can you help my baby sista n' me
make it through another night?
See our Daddy's in jail for hurting a man,
and our mama's on the pipe.

Lord, this won't be a very long letter.
I'm tired, from putting the baby to sleep.
She was crying because she's hungry
see, we don't have any food to eat.

Grandma wants us to come live with her.
She says, this is no place for children to be.
But Mama don't want to lose this check
she gets for my sista and me.

Lord, I really don't like those men who curse
my mama, or the things she let's them do
And I'm so afraid sometimes
When they try to touch me too!

Well, Lord, I have to go now
My sista's crying again.
I try to do my best for her,
But you know, I'm only ten.

Dear Lord!
Can you help my baby sista n' me
make it through another night?
See our Daddy's in jail for hurting a man,
and our mama's on the pipe.

Please Lord, if you find time
won't you bring our mama back.
We were so much happier
before she started smokin' crack!
I love you!

The Mighty Right

They cursed him and they called him names,
Still he carried the burden of
envious blame.
It was evil thoughts that filled their heads.
He had done no wrong, still they
Wanted him dead.
Yes, the son of God was charged with being less than a man
They called for his death
Pilate washed his hands.
He said, take him among you, do what you will.
I'll have no part of Calvary Hill — or your
Jesus, The Mighty Right What was done to wrong
The mighty light
He was Jesus, The Mighty Right.
They made him carry that cross through the streets;
They nailed his feet.
Yet he still said a prayer, before the day was through
He said, "forgive Them, Father,
They know not what they do."
Jesus left so we might know our sins
Then on the third day
He returned again.
He said the way is lit, to your Father's door;
Faith is the key; you need no more.
He told them; What has been said is what is to be,
I speak not, God speaks through me."
He is Jesus, The Mighty Light
What was done to wrong
Jesus, The Mighty Right.

Thank God For Jesus

Wonderful Counselor
The only begotten Son
Prince of Peace
The One and Only One.

I Thank God for Jesus.
He Suffered and Died for Us.
Thank God for Jesus
For in His Love We Trust.
Thank God for Jesus.

He's The Lamb of God
Who Died and Rose Again
To Redeem the World
From a Multitude of Sin.

He's My Personal Savior.
He's Good, Merciful and Kind
The Way, The Truth, and The Light;
He's My Savior Divine.

Wonderful Counselor
The Only Begotten Son
Prince of Peace
The One and Only One.

One Who Baptizes in the Spirit
The Light of Life, Messiah, and Friend
"The Alpha and the Omega
The Beginning and the End".

I Thank God for Jesus
He suffered and Died For Us.
Thank God for Jesus
For In His Love We Trust.
Thank God for Jesus.

God Love Is...
Still on the Throne

It matters not
What we call him by name
Cuz in the spirit of love
We're all one in the same.

With clothes on my back
Shoes on my feet, and food on the table
Just call him up
I know, God is able.

God's love is still
On the throne
And as long as
You do his will
He'll never leave
You alone
God's love is still
On the throne.

Just remember no matter
What you're goin' thru
Up lift your faith in God
And to your self be true.

God is still
Blessin' the world
With all his devine worth
Gave his one and only son
That we might someday
Have peace on earth.

In a world that seem
Much too cold, cruel
And just ugly to the bone
The Widsom, warmth
And Wonder of God's love
Can melt a heart of stone.

With clothes on my back
Shoes on my feet, And food on my table
Just call him up
I know, God is able.

God's love is still
On the Throne
And as long as
You do his will
He'll never leave
You alone
For God's love is still
On the throne.

Just-Family

Black-Love

Black on Black Love
is a weapon of war.
Ain't no time to
Sleep walk thru life anymore.

Brother To Brother

When it comes
to you and me,
Brother to Brother,
That's the way
it's supposed to be
cuz there's a part of you
that lives in me,
Brother to Brother.

THE WOL Family Poem
A Tribute to Cathy Hughes

As Queen Mother of 1450
WOL and MAGIC 102.3
You are the voice of information
And power for the WOL Family.

As a Radio-Activist
For the Whole Black-Nation
You are the soul-source of so much
Life givin' information.

And I love you so much more
Than words can ever say
'Cause you offer love in a
Very special kinda way.

You offer home-grown
Love with a heart to heal
Any bad-blood between us
That we sometimes feel.

So whether ridin' in your car
Or just chillin' at home
Don't touch that dial
No, just leave it alone.

If you wanna WWIN
Leave it where it ought to be
On the big WOL, and MAJIC
One oh two point three.

Some say you're a master
Motor mouth, but I really don't mind
Cuz when it comes to givin' us what
We need, you're always right on time.

The power of information
Is knowledge and you never
Fail to keep us informed.
Even if it means bendin'
Over backwards, you fly into
The very eye of the storm.

And I love you so much more
Than words can simply say
'Cause you offer love in a
Spiritually-special kinda way.

So just let the news
Music and information flow
From the"We Offer Love" family
On the Cathy Hughes Mornin' Show.

Brother Ta Brother

I turn to you
and you are there for me
with understanding, for that with
even I do not understand about myself.

Though I'm older in years
I am student of your learning
it is said wisdom knows
not time.

It is a true blessing
to have been given one
such as you, for you are
an inspiration to my
heart and mind

and Brother to Brother
I Love You.

To A Father and A Friend

Ever since I can remember,
and even before then,
you have always been there for me,
as a father and a friend.
Like all the times in the past,
when life seemed so unfair
and I needed to know which way to go,
With understanding, you were always there.

You have also shared my joyous times
Like the joy I feel today
A joy filled with love for you
in so very many ways.

I LOVE YOU FATHER
with a love so deep and true
and just as you have been there for me
I will always be here for you!
God Bless You!

Dear Daddy
I love you

I really miss you
and all the stuff we used to do
so I just had to write and ask you
Daddy, do you miss me too?

I would love for you to call me
and let me know you're doing fine
Because with so many bad things happening
I worry about you sometimes.

Mama says you have a problem
and that's all that she will say,
so every night when I pray to God
I ask him to take your problem away.

Oh Daddy, I'm still doing good in school,
but my teacher thinks I can do more.
And I'm saving all my report cards,
so I can show you all my scores.

I know grow-ups sometimes have problems
that children don't understand,
But it's just not the same since you're not here
Please come home as soon as you can.

Now don't you forget to call me soon
Our number is still the same.
Remember, I love you Daddy
And that will never change.

Nation-Time

Message To The Blackman For the Honorable Elijah Muhammad

From the original man
To the brotherhood of mankind
If you trust in the truth
You can unlock your mind.

When you know who you are
You can stand up for yourself
For the knowledge of truth
Won't let you be nobody else.

So in the name of Allah
This is a message
To the Blackman in America.

Man to man, I hope you
Feel the same way I do.
Brother to brother, there's a part
Of me that lives for you.

Heart to heart, soul to soul
Native son to native son
With a common sense of self
You're second to none.

So in the name of Allah
This is a message
To the Blackman in America.

Black Self-Respect
(A Poem For My People)

Self respect can only
come from a sense of self
it's not somethin' you get
from somebody else.

When you know who you are
beyond all self-denial and doubt
self love, and self respect can only
come from the inside out.

It's not somethin' anyone else
can give you or simply take away
self respect is a gift from the creator
that's always with you to stay.

From the kingdom of heaven within
and the universal-mind above,
black self respect is the essence
of black self-love.

When you know who you are
beyond all self denial and doubt
self-love and self respect can only
come from the inside out.

Malcolm
The Man Behind the X

Some folk will always say
This, That, and the other
But for the love of his people
Malcolm was a true to life brother.

Malcolm The Man Behind
The Message, was a native son
Of the man behind the mission
They call the Most Honorable One.

The true X factor of Malcolm X
And the Principle behind the man
Can never be simply X'd out
By the power of the unseen hand.

As a prophet of black pride
And black militancy
Malcolm was our guiding light
Of self-respect and integrity.

Unmoved and unshaken
By those still on the plantation
Malcolm was a master-mind
Of the Lost Found Nation.

With strong convictions
And a character simply-complex
Everybody's got their own ideas
About the man behind the X.

Malcolm was a scholar from the streets
A black man of principle and good
Who came to restore the true
Nature of black-manhood.

In the moral ethics of life
And Black self-love
Brother Malcolm has a Ph.D.
And in the art of speaking to
The heart, the man behind the X
Had a Master's degree.

He had an uncanny ability
To speak what was on his mind
And as an orator of raw-power
He was our spiritual lifeline.

And as long as white supremacy
Is forever firmly rooted
The man behind the X can never
Be X'd out or excluded.

Through his spiritual, cultural
And political self as livin' proof
Brother minister was no sell-out
He was committed to the truth.

And with strong convictions
And a personality simply-complex
He was one of the chosen ones
Brother Malcolm: The Man Behind The X.

Eatin' To Live

Eat one balanced meal
A day, no need for more
eat only when hungry
but never before.

Learn how to eat to live
You will find true wealth
cuz ain't no price tag on
peace of mind and good health.

Pigin' Out

The high you get from
Hog-Heaven is a done deal.
Some folk spend a life time
pigin out at the Hogs on the Hill.

The way you eat
and what you eat
is a down-right disgrace
gotta be more mindful
of just how and what
you feed your face.

The make-up of the pig
is the rat,the cat, and the dog
But Rev. Chicken-Wing
and Bishop-Pork Chop
are too high on the hog
To make themselves stop.

The Devil's diet of Death
is for the strong and the Brave
eatin on the run, and runnin' on
a pig's foot, will run you to your grave.

Pigin out on Bacon
Sausage, chitterling and ham
and too high on death
To really give a damn.

When there's a poisonous
swine odor all in the air
you can bet there a bar-be-cue
hog cookin somewhere.

On the smell of smoke-pig
you feel like you can just fly
But some folk spend a life-time
pigin' out on a hog-head high.

The right way to eat
will prolong life and give
more life abundancy,
yet the eating of Mr. Pig
Mr. Hog, and Mr. Swine is
more deadly than H.l.V.

So the Devil's diet of Death
is for the strong and the Brave
cuz eatin' on the run, and running on
a pig's foot, will run you in your grave.

Dollars "n" Sense

You can have yours
Just as the man's got his
When you put your money
Where your mouth is...

Dollars "N" Sense
Can really mean a lot
When we come together
With all we've got.

 Do yourself a favor
And take stock in your own
The Dollars "N" Cents of black money
Must begin at home.

For the sake of some
 "In God we trust"
Everybody believes in the power
 Of black money except us.

To stop being the economic
 Doormat of everybody else
We gotta learn to do
Something for self.

Unlock your mind
You can still be free
From the Psychological chains
Of Economic slavery.

If you believe in black ice
Despite all you've been told
You must invest in your own
Black-gold.

You can have yours
Just as the man's got his
When you put your money
Where your mouth is...

Dollars "N" Sense
Can really mean a lot
When we come together
With all we've got.

So don't short change yourself
To invest in everybody else
For in all that you do
Why not invest in you.

Nation Time

The bitter truth of a
Rude-awakening from a
plantation state of mind
is the cause and effect
of what conscious folk
call nation-time.

Wake-Up Call: The Final Call
A Tribute to
Hon. Min. Louis Farrakhan

Wake up, to the truth
And simply unlock your mind.
Those who heed the final call
Are those that know the time.

Nothin' comes to dreamers
Too weak to stand tall
Nothin' comes to sleepers
Who dream much too small.

Wake up to who you are
The handwriting's on the wall
Wake up, and smell the coffee
For this is the final call.

Ain't no where to run
Nowhere to duck n' dodge
Everywhere you look, massa Charlie
Is still in charge.

We gotta wake up, and stop
Looking to somebody else
For what we truly need
Is a new sense of self.

Wake up to who you are
And simply unlock your mind.
Those who heed the final call
Are those that know the time.

Beyond the shadow
Of all we've been through
An unconditional love of self
Is somewhere deep inside of you.

Wake up, to the truth of who you are
The handwritings on the wall
Wake up and smell the coffee
For this is the final call.

The Most Honorable One

With a superior-sense of self
And a third grade education
He gave us a blu-print to
A self-lovin' nation.

For the love of his people
His life givin' teachin's are
Simply second to none
The Messenger of Allah, was the
Lamb of life they called
The Most Honorable one.

With Qur'an in one hand
And Bible in the other
Allah is God, in full control
He made the messenger an Apostle
Of self knowledge, and a prophet
Of food for the soul.

His mission in life
Was divinely inspired
For his people, and no one else
To help the black man
In American do somethin'
For self.

He taught universal truth
Thru the technology of time
He knew the blackman and woman
So well, He was a Supreme-Master-Mind.

With the mighty F.O.I and M.G.T.
As his right and left arm
He gave breath of life to the
Lost-Found Nation of Islam.

Yet in the name of deceit
And self hate, the work of
The devil is never done
But nothin' can up-root
The seeds of success planted
By the most honourable one.

With a superior sense of self
And a third grade education
He gave us a blu-print
To a self lovin' nation.

Thus the fore-sight of the man
Behind the message, and the mission
Will give you the insight
You need to stand tall
When the last trumpet of truth
Sounds the Final Call.

Food for Thought

Walkie - Talkie

You can turn a dyin'ember
Into a full fledged, flame of fire
And when it comes to somebody else's
Business, you're a real live wire.

No Deposit; No Return

To whom it may concern:
As we live Love and Learn
Where there's No Deposit
There can be No Return.

Big Ben

After Robin' Peter to Pay Paul
I ended-up doin' Big-Ben
with my back against the wall.
Brought into a bad-bill of goods
and now I finally found out
it's really not worth it at all.

Slick Sly And The Wicked
For Slick Willie

You are affronted the rain-bow Folk
and Sista-Souljah in the name of race,
But like always, you are the master of
white-tradition in black face.

Melanin On My Mind
Tribute To Dr. Frances
Cress Welsing

Those with lack of livin' color
Seek a darker shade of sunshine
But ain't no-thang to me
I've got Melanin on my mind.

Melanin is the chemical key
To a pure pro-black state of mind.
The down-play of a sense of self
Is of mindless master design.

Melanin, the cosmic key
To the colors by far
Is the power and essence
Of who we really are.

With insights of innervision
Trust in the truth, and understand
A natural high, is the brainchild
Of the pineal gland.

Through the third eye
Or the pineal gland
Self-love, is self-knowledge
With an open hand...
But it's a" black thang
Some folk wouldn't understand".

Melanin, the cosmic key
To the colors by-far
Is the power and essence
Of who we really are.

The mindful people of Melanin
Are most simply second to none.
There's a color conscious, cosmic connection
To the true children of the sun.

Those with lack of livin' color
Seek a darker shade of sunshine
But ain't no-thang to me
I've got Melanin on my mind.

Depends On What You Read?

I write about the other side,
but that depends which side you're on?
I write about injustice,
and how it's been going on too long.

I write about the body count
due to the lack-of- law in the streets;
I write about children living in the nation's
capital, who don't even have food to eat.

I write about the part of town
only the residents needs;
I write about a lot of things
Depends on what you read?

I write about mass unemployment
in a land saturated with Hy-Tech;
I write about the cost of the war,
that hasn't been paid for yet.

I write about The North American Trade Agreement,
and it's underlying policy of greed;
I write about a lot of things;
Depends on what you read?

I write about Bosnia, Somalia
and even Uncle Sam's new right-hand-man;
I write about the Klu Klux Klan,
but who gives a damn?

I write about this world,
which is trouble indeed;
I write about a lot of things
Depends on what you read?

Lip Service

False pride can never
Truly make you proud
If all you ever do is
Say nothin' and talk
Real loud.

A Hero at Heart

To get to know
The you nobody knew
Is to play it smart
Cuz you're a born survivor
A hero at heart.

Trust your heart
And you can win
For the power of the
Higher self, will surely
Teach you how to be
Your own best friend.

It pays to discover
The inner essence of self
Cuz there's a world of difference
Between you 'n' somebody else.

So if you would
Only to your self
Be ever so true
There's a hero at
Heart, that lives
inside of you.

Admirations

Beauty Beyond Control
For Janet Jackson

You are the pure essence
of black beauty, beyond control
Somethin' about you just moves
My heart, all the way to my soul.

I love Loving You

From the day I asked your name
never, never was it a game.
Believe me, nothing's been the same.
Lady, I love loving you.

I was yours from the start.
You hold the key to my happy heart
There's no way we could ever part.

You're my midnight shining star
oh what you do, to my heart
So beautiful to me you are.

And it thrills me through & through
All the thoughtful things you do.
Lady, I love loving you.

Baby, you'll always have my best
My all and nothing less.
In love's school, we've passed the test.

And it thrills me through & through
To you, I'll always be true.
And lady, oh lady, say lady
Lady, I love loving you.

No Sell Out

I've been lost n' found
here and there, and round about,
but I just found me
and I ain't no sell out.

So trust your heart
and trust in me
self love ain't somethin'
you get for free.

I'm livin' proof that things
Ain't always what they seem
I was so caught up in livin'
somebody else's dream.

I was lost n' found
here and there, and round about,
But I just found me
and I ain't no sell out.

The Happy Birthday Poem

Think of this day as if it
Were a letter to your heart
With your soul in mind.
For what you have given
To so many, is a sense of self
To last the course of a lifetime.

And like Afrikan sunrise
You warm my heart to no end;
When I was down and out
You showed me how to live again.

But for the love of life
You are some kind of wonderful
In each and every way;
And in the name of love
The very thought of you
Simply says this is your day.
Happy Birthday.

Mothers From the Motherland Sista to Sister: For Susan L. Taylor

To rise and shine
live in the light and succeed
A self accepting, can do attitude
is all we really need.

For the sake of sisterly love
and the timeless ties that bind,
a new vision of hope
will give us a new mind.

Beyond all hopelessness
despair, and master control,
Mothers from the Motherland
are sistas of the soul.

When we shape the future
in our own image to make a new start
we can build bridges of hope
to each others heart.

Only faith and love
can make us what we ought to be
heart to heart-in the spirit
a call for conscious unity.

And sista to sister
soul to soul, hand in hand
we are one with the hearts
Of mothers from the motherland!

Mother Nature

The love of life
is wrapped up in
the thorn and the rose
and all the true ways
of Mother Nature
no man really knows.

Chocolate City Candy

Just a taste of you
Makes my life so complete
Learnin to love you
Is a special treat.

The little lovin' things you do
Forever makes you honey sweet,
Your Good 'n' Plenty lovin'
Just knocks me off my feet.

You're my Sugar Baby
Peppermint-Pattie Pearl
My M&M Plain, Chocolate City
Candy Girl.

My lifetime, Life Saver
Fifth Avenue, Lover's Lane Park
My Butterfingered, whatchamacallit
Such sweetness in the dark.

Now and later you'll always
Be my Mary jane, my Baby Ruth
My Mounds of Almonds Joy
Chocolate honey sweet tooth.

Let me be your Payday
Sugar Daddy galore
Your one 100 Grand
Mr. Goodbar for sure.

When your turn on your total
Tootsie Roll charm,
Your chocolate cherry kisses
Make me melt in your arms.

You're my Sugar Baby
Peppermint-Pattie Pearl.
My M&M Plain, Chocolate City
Candy Girl

The Body Bag Blues

Thumbs Down (To The Beam)

Walking in this house
first thing I see
a dirty faced kid
starin'up at me.

Tear stained eyes
his hair's a mess
But yo, you, wait a second
while I tell you the rest.

His clothes need changin'
wearin' one dirty sock
too young to know
his mama's on the rock.

Forsakin' family & friends
so it seems
And puttin' their whole heart
In the very next beam.

And what's the first thing they want
when the rocks all gone
first another blast
then a shoulder ta cry on.

But Scotty's done all the dirt
he could do to me
I got my body back
I got my family.

So thumbs down to the beam
you know what I mean
never, ever to forget
How good it feels to be clean.

Say you wanna stop
But you're in too deep
Makin' all the small promises
you never seem to keep.

You want the life you had
before you started to smoke
Well if it ain't no joke
Yeah stop, don't take another take!

One no at a time
That's the thing to do
see, you're the only body
who can do it for you.

Helpin' each other that's
what it's really about
Help me, Help you
And let's shout it out.

Scotty, you've done all the dirt
you could do to me
I want my body back
I want my family back.

Thumbs down to your beam
sure you know what I mean
It feels so goooood
to finally be clean.

The White Girl
A Tribute to Tony Brown

The White Girl is nothing
But a Street-Wise name
For a Shady-Lady called
Crack Coke-cane.

The love of the White-Lady
Is an unnatural high
A halo of self-hatred
That keeps you living a lie.

For all hue-man life is a
Precious, priceless pearl
Without the self-destructive
Mind Set of the White Girl.

But a whole lot of self-love
Is the Brain-Child of high self-esteem
To help you resist the power
Of this Lily-White Queen.

A SOULJAH'S STORY
A Salute to Sister-Souljah

For the love of
Sistuh-Souljah,
activist, raptivist
Queen-Mother Bee,
A voice for the voiceless
At war for conscious unity.

As Queen-Warrior
Of the hip-hop nation,
Souljah is on the battlefield
for black liberation.

Like P.R.T., krs-one
X clan and B.D.P.,
Sister-Souljah is America's
number one public enemy.

So before you judge a book
better turn the page
Rappers are the new teachers
Preachers and prophets of rage.

In essence
of her namesake
thru courage and commitment
she's got what it takes.

Souljah, is a soul-trooper
a born survivor from the hood
who was not born to make
white folk feel good.

From her heart to her people
Sister-Souljah gives her all,
and we can't let political hype
push her back against the wall.

As queen-mother warrior
of the hip-hop nation,
Souljah is on the battlefield
for black liberation.

With just-us and truth
as her only claim to glory,
I sing the praises of a true
(no-sell out) Souljah's story.

As a real to life rebel
of rhyme and reason,
you give spiritual food to
African minds for all seasons.

The media lords of deception
have only just begun,
But the blessings of the ancestors
will help us do what must be done.

So before you judge the book
better turn the page
rappers are the new poets
preachers and prophets of rage.

GUNS SMOKE

and another youth dies
His friends pay respect
while his mother cries - "why"?
Avenging a friend or deal gone bad
Killed for the love of a girl he'll never have.

Guns Smoke!

In the papers everyday.
When you gonna stop
carryin' yourself that way?
You're bigger than that
or so you profess,
but your actions don't make you
no bigger then the rest.

Guns Smoke!

For who's number this time?
the kid's, fourteen and he's packin' a "g".
Dead in the streets
another body lies
Shot from the window,
of a car that drove by.

Guns Smoke!

And you think you're boss;
you need to go find
the mind you lost!
If you put the tool down
and stop sellin' the crack,
You might use your head for more
than just tottin' a hat.
Think! who's gonna care for
the babies you've made
when you're in the penitentiary
or dead in a grave?

Gun Smoke!

To the Uptown Mob,
and the Downtown Crew
Stop lettin' the dollar bill,
make an ass outta you.
In your respect for your "tech"
You'll die or live to regret
Forever tryin' to catch-up; You see,
the courts are crowded
and the morgue is too
and they just gettin' richer
because of people like you;

Guns Smoke!

And another youth dies;
His friends pay their last respect,
as his broken hearted mother cries
"why" — "why"?

The Body-Bag Blues
(Black-hand in white Glove)

Until we learn to love
Who we are in our own reflection
Self-hate, is a deadend street
With no direction.

When caught up
And wrapped up
In the body-bad blues
If you're livin' the life
Sooner or later, you gonna
Have to pay some dues.

I get so sick n' tired
Of the street-life blues
Another senseless killin'
It's the same old bad news.

A drive shootin'
Ain't nothin' but a direct
Hit and run
And another Blackman dies
But nobody ever talks about
Who's bringin' in the drugs n' guns.

The buy-product
Of drugs is violence
And it's at an all time high
Black on black love
Like black self-respect
Is in short-supply.

For powerlessness can make
Any man feel, only half alive
Cuz the so called war on drugs
Ain't nothin' but black genocide.

And as long as Amerika, is Amerika
There will always be a ...
Black hand in white-glove
But passion for life
Can only be found in the power
Of self love.

Every time I turn on
The one eyed monster
With the tail in the back
No news is good news
It's brothers killin' brothers
Black on Black.

So let me put just
One thing on your mind
White folk could care less
When we kill our own kind.

Sistas n' brothas of the soul
Are takin' each other out
Over somethin' dumb
And the cold blooded reality
Of takin' another hue-man life
Can only make the spirit numb.

So until we learn to love
Who we are in our own reflection
Self-hate is a dead end street
With no direction.

Cuz as long as Amerika, is Amerika
There will always be a
Black hand in a white glove
But true passion for life
Can only be found in the power
Of self love.

For there can only be perfect
Peace in the valley of the hood
When we love who we are
For the sake of our own good.

Weekend State of Mind

By the time the weekend
Has finally come to town
All I can say is stop the world
I wanna get off, this merry go round.

A full daze work
Is a full days pay
But too much over time
Is all work and no play.

For two days outa seven
I'm happy 'n' home free
From the stress 'n' strain
Of a dead end J.O.B.

It pays the bills
Tho it's less than
A labor of love
But I'm not complaining
Cuz all blessings come from above.

I've waited all
Week long just to say
The weekend is here
And thank God it's Friday.

The work week is over
I've paid my dues
And I've done my time
The eagles flys on Friday
And I'm in a weekend
State of mind.

When pay day Friday
Has finaly come 'round
I'm so very happy
I could kiss the ground.

Come what may
I don't get caught up
In the mind games
People sometimes play.

The mental paralysis
Of makin' the ends meet
The simple bottom line
Will keep you chained 'n' bound
When workin' on a planation
Of the mind.

Come blue Monday
Ready or not, like it or not
I'll do it all again
Cuz from nine to five
Monday thru Friday
I'm in the lion's den.

So until Friday
Rolls around, I'm livin'
For the bottom line
Cuz if the truth be known
When at work I'm always
In a weekend state of mind.

Memories

There are those special memories
We cherish through the years;
Most of them are happy ones,
But some are filled with tears.

They all become more beautiful
The older that they grow,
And with their age they take their place
As days of long ago.

They are the pictures of a past
For which we sometimes yearn,
But which we know so well is gone
And which cannot return.

They have no marked value
In our commerce of today;
They are not even anything
That we can give away.

And yet the memories can play
A most important part
As they inspire or console
Or otherwise help the heart.

Just-Us

Just-Us Denied
For Terrance Johnson

When and Where There's
No true truths, we can trust
The double standard of Justice
Simply means Just-us.

Liberty and Justice for all
in America is only based on
money, sex and race,
but the injustice of just-us
in America ain't nothin'
But a basket-case.

Somehow mad-dog justice
is the law of the land
and they really don't mind
Justice being denied, A black man.

In a moment of truth
Just-us denied, only
means me and you
But it's a tug-of-war
with Justice only for
a chosen few.

Just-us delayed
is Justice-gone taboo
For just-us denied
For justice too long over due.

What is it, in this
So called law of the land
That makes my life less valuable
Than that of a police-man.

A protocol-prisoner
is sentenced for life
by the wicked-ways of the wild bunch,
but injustice goes unpunished
simply becauz the judge and jury
are all out to lunch.

Systematic-institutional
Injustice, is a weapon of war
so how can a Black man be free
when what they call justice
rests only in the hands
of his open enemy.

So.. Just -us delayed
is justice-gone ta-boo
for just-us denied
is Justice too long over-due.

Jes-us Deferred
A Tribute to D.C Mayor
Marion Barry

Cut him low
And hang him high,
But if this is what is what you call justice
We're all just livin' a lie.

Top secret, selective enforcement
Is the true law of the land
Especially when it comes to
The lynchin' of a blackman.
As the United Snakes of Amerika
Seeks to checkmate, the mayor
Lynch law justice is the very
Essence of bein unfair.

Mother media over kill
Is forever workin' overtime
With a venomous purple-poison
To keep shackels on our minds.

Lights, camera, and action
Right before our very eyes,
But I'm fed up with the feds
And their head-hunting lies.
Steeped in sex-opera alibis
When what comes out from undercover
Is far from a pleasant surprise.

A little smoke, and a little drink
Is admittedly self-proclaimed
But entrapment is injustice
By any other name
So the hunter gets captured
By the real life to game.

The persecution of Mayor Barry
Is simply beast like, at it's best
But the federal guard-dogs on duty
Would never settle for anything less.

Who's right, who's wrong?
Ain't no need to worry

'Cause there ain't no justice
For D.C. Mayor Marion Barry.
And as long as injustice is the
Double standard of the day,
The collective federal white-wolves
Will have it their way
With the Cu-Clux, cut throat
Tactics of the F.B.I. and the C.l.A.

For top secret entrapment
Is the true law of the land
Especially when it comes to
The crucifixion of a blackman.

So cut him real low
And hang him sky high
But if this is what you call justice
We're all just livin' a lie.

Plantation Psychosis
A Tribute to Dr. Naim Akbar

From miseducation to education
Is a sense of sight of all time
To unlearn all that you've learned
Is a true revolution of the mind.

Stolen legacies of self love
And the lack of Hue-man pride
Is made manifest by chains and images
Of psychological suicide.

A color blind love is a sight
for some sore eyes to see
'Cause love comes in all colors
to those who sleep with the enemy.

For the white stamp of approval
The modern Tom would give his right arm
And end up a half hearted has been
on the white Folks Funny-Farm.

The wicked ways of white folks
won't give you no self lovin' space
You gotta do what you're told
Boy, you gotta stay in your place.

A jelly-back, weak-kneed, hallow-headed
Hamburger eatin', house negro
Ain't nothin' but a state of the art
stool pigeon, for the sake of the status quo.

And a color blind love is a sight
For some sore eyes to see
'Cause love comes in all colors
To those who sleep with the enemy

Take an oreo-minded Uncle Tom
Who wants to be what he is not
And a misdirected make believe
Blackman is all you've really got.

More white than white folks
In all that you do say
A carbon copy of craziness
But it ain't gotta be that way.

AIN'T NO JUSTICE
The Rodney King Poem

What went on in the dark
Has finally come to light
The whole-world saw what you did
And it just ain't right.

What went down in LA
In the Rodney King case
Was a psychological awakening
For the whole hue-man race.

After the fire and the fury
Who's gonna take the weight
'Cause the city of angels
Is in a hell of a state.

The fraternal order of four L.A.P.D. pigs
Should never go scott-free
When caught in a clear act
Of police brutality.

Everytime I think of what
Happened to Rodney King in LA
My whole life flashes before me
In an instant replay.

What went on in the dark
Has finally come to light
The whole-world saw what you did
And it just ain't right.

So anytime I'm stopped
By a cop, I just chill
And give the utmost respect
To the man with a license to kill.

Until police brutality
And outright injustice cease
America, the so call beautiful
Will never have any peace.

What the system calls justice
Ain't nothin' but a fine mess
And in truth, I don't want no part of
What they call due-process.

Justice in America has tested
Positive for H.I.V.
and there's a malignant cancer
Called white-supremacy.

When you know that justice
has never been served
to look the undisputed truth
In the face, it takes a lotta nerve.

So anytime I'm stopped
By a cop, I just chill
But how can I respect
The man with a license to kill?

When what went on in the dark
Has finally come to light
The whole-world saw what you did
And it just ain't right.

CR 24/7 X 9

No Norplant

Don't give up
Body nor soul
To the unseen hand
Of remote control.

A rude awakening
To Truth can cut
Like a knife,
But to me the side-effects
Of ignorance can
Cost you your life.

Know your enemy
And know your self
Inside-out, and outside-in
Don't let what they call
Common sense get
Down under your skin.

Don't give up
Body nor Soul
To the unseen hand
Of remote control.

Booty in the Bottle

Gay, Lesbian, or somewhere
In between
It just ain't my way of life,
If you know what I mean.

The show and tell
Kiss and tell lifestyle
Of sleepin round-a-bout
is like a taste of ta-boo booty
Behind closet doors and
livin in a glass house.

All I know is
Woman is woman
And Man is man
For anything less than that
Was not apart of...
The Master's plan.

Gay-Bi-or straight
Family, friend or foe
It broke me up to find out
That a honey named sugar
Was a Lesbo.

If you close your eyes
To truth, you can
never see the light
Becuz the things people
Sometimes do. For what they
So-call love, just ain't right.

You don't chose to be
Born black or white
But you can choose to be gay
Therefore honey-bun rights
And Civil-rights are like
Night and Day.

So if I could take all
The gay and Lesbo booty
That's already on display
And put it in a bottle
I'd simply label it
happy doesn't mean gay.

To get a real charge
'Outa love, you gotta have
A nut and a screw,
And anything other
Than what's really real
Just can't be true.

The show and tell
Kiss and tell life style
Of sleepin' round-a-bout
Is like a taste of Ta-boo booty
Behind close doors and
Living in a glass house.

But if you could sometimes
See yourself the way others do
And not be selfishly head-strong
Maybe then, you could
Give your-self, the right
To be dead wrong.

Why

Little people, I need a hand
To make grow-ups understand
They're endangerin you and me,
But it's hard for them to see.

Life is moving so fast
And before another day passes
Pull one grown-up aside
Look them in the eye
And ask them to explain; Why?

Why-So many people starve?
Why-So many don't have jobs?
Why-So much war?
Why-Can't they do a little more?

There are so many of you
So there's a chance you might break through
To help ease their minds
In these troubled times
If you'll just ask - why?

Why bombs are such a threat?
Why haven't they stopped making them yet?
Why they argue about prayer in school
Why they've forgotten the Gold Rule?
Why all this Black-White thing?
Why remember Dr. King?

All we really want to know is - why?
Little friends, you see your job
and I know it's going to be hard,
But they need you now
And maybe somehow
They can tell you why?

Why the lack of family ties?
Why TV often lies?
Why teachers are underpaid?
Why faith in God continues to fade?
All we really need to know is why?
Why?

White Supremacy
A tribute to Dr. Frances
Welsing & Mr Neely Fuller

As Long as white supremacy
Is alive and well,
A white man's heaven
Is a black man's hell.

Uncle Sam and Jim Crow
Are the archdeceivers of the game
And that old skinhead, Ku Klux spirit,
Is still the same.

As a manchild of the sun
I've got melanin on my mind
Can't afford to be simply
Deaf, Dumb and Blind
When white supremacy
Is the bottom line.

And as long as white supremacy
Is alive and still kickin' ass,
Freedom, Justice and Equality
Will never come to pass.

Many look, but only
Few ever really see
The most unjust dynamic
In the world is white supremacy.

The Cress theory of color
Conscious confrontation
Is about the fear of white
Genetic annihilation.

Too white to be black
Too black To be white in this man's land
For the way of the white minded
Negro is a part of the master plan.

The Chess Board of white supremacy
Will pull the game of real life over our eyes
'Cause the wishy-washy ways of white folk
Are the ways of the wickedly-wise.

But when we know the sum
Total of our sense of self,
We sure can't afford
To be nobody else.

And as long as white supremacy
Is alive and well,
A white man's heaven
Is a black man's hell.

For Many look, but only
Few ever really see
The most unjust dynamic
In the world is white supremacy.

The Loose-Booty Blues
A Safe-Sex Poem

I was standing on the verge of gettin' it on
When I heard the news
'Bout Mr. Magic's intercourse
With the Loose Booty Blues.

A greedy man caught in the act
With a sex-machine mind
Might be doin' it to death
For the very last time.

But it's your thang
Do what you want
But, do what you must
'Cause when it cums to safe-sex
Ain't nobody you can trust.

So before you end up on a
Dead-end street, with no direction
Take these words of heed
For your own protection.

Every-Body that looks good
May not be good in fact
And ain't it funky now
How a prisoner of free-love
Can be caught in the act.

Let sexual-ethics
And sexual-discipline be
The lifeline to true love today
To stop this intercourse with death
It's got to be that way.

Ain't nowhere to run
'Cause you sure can't hide;
You got to be tried
Tested and found true
On the negative side.

Caught up in the courtesy
Of moonlight magic and
livin the life
The sweet-temptations of sex
Without love is nothing but
A fool's paradise.

But it's your thang
Do what you want
But, do what you must
'Cause when it cums to safe-sex
Ain't nobody you should trust.

So before you end up on a
Dead-end street, with no direction
Take these words of heed
For your own protection.

Babies Making Babies

Some Kids Are Just A Pain
Morning, Night, And Noon
Some Kids Never Grow Up
Others Grow Up All Too Soon.

With A New Birth In Her Arms
And Another At Her Side
They're All That She Has
To Give Her A Sense Of Pride.

Stop This Wheel Of Shame
Stop This Wheel Of Pain
Baby Ain't Got No Name
Don't Know Who's To Blame.

Babies Making Babies
Where Do We Draw The Line
Babies Having Babies
It's A Sign Of The Times
Babies Making Babies.

You Say When You Get That Feeling
You Just Got To Do It
But Oh, Let Me Tell You Child
In Real Life There's So Much More To It.

And Whether It's A Lovable Lad
Or A Priceless Baby Girl
This Ain't No Cabbagepatch Kid
You're Bringing Into The World.

When It Comes To Life And Love
Tell Me Why Can't You See
That Love Carries With it
A Sense of Pride, And Responsibility.

Hooked On The Labor Of Love
You Gave Into A Feeling Unknown
And After Motherhood The Hard Way
You know, Love Don't Live By Sex Alone.

StopThis Wheel Of Shame
Stop This Wheel Of Pain
Baby ain't got no name
Don't know who's to blame.

Babies Making Babies
Where Do We Draw The Line
Babies Having Babies
It's A Sign Of The Times
Babies Making Babies.

Aids
The Master

I've analyzed the situation
I've thought about it through and through
And I think you should call me "The Master"
for what I do to you.

Oh let me tell you my real name
before you start to laugh;
I'm the one you people call Aids
And you don't want to cross my path.

For if you do I'll make you a believer
Of all the things you don't believe;
you see once I check into your body
You can be sure, I'll never leave.

Many people have died from me
some you probably knew;
And now I'll wait for you to slip-up
So I can get you too.

Now through research they've found a way
To kind of slow me down;
Some have died while trying to kill me
But you see I'm still around.

Yes I'm all the things you've heard I am
All that you've been told;
yes I'm also color-blind
So I don't waste my time on skin;
You work on the racial points
While I work-out within.

So just keep doing, what you're doing
And I just might see you around;
I've been traveling all over the world
But now I'm living in your town.

Band-Aids Blues

Don't expect
A dying man
To get well soon
If all you're done
is put a Band-Aid
on a gun-shot wound.

Soul-foo yung

Some say, they don't speak
English and don't understand
A single word we say
At least, not until you
Have what you want, and it's
Time for you to pay.

Before they take yo' money
At times, they can be
Just nicer than nice
And at other times
They can be down right
Rude and very impolite.

We seem to have a
Sweet 'n' sour love, for chinese food
Beyond concious-control
But a taste of self love, minus
A side order of self ignorance
Is food for the soul.

But come and get it
So called, soul-foo yung
With a combination treat
Come and get it
Hot n' Spicey, insult with injury
All you can eat

To come together
And pull together
As one, Is our master-key
Because it's time for a
Rude-awakenin' in the black
Community.

Everybody loves to eat
But nobody likes to cook
That's why Papa-Sung is on
Everycorner, every where you look.

There's no outlet
For self-love in a carryout
Own'd by someone else
Why not, open a place of business
Call it, Soul foo Yung
And do somethin' for self.

Time out, for tasteless
Economic appetizers
With no main course or entree
The blackman, Is the very salt
and seasonin' of all life
It's time for a new and better day.

But come and get it,
So called, soul-foo cuisine
With a combination treat
Come and get it
Hot n' Spicy, Insult with Injury
All you can eat.

The Cycle

Every twenty eight
or thirty days at a time
life can cramp your style
and play tricks on your mind.

To be quite blunt
and right up front
everyday is Mother's Day
Once every month.

The many moods
of P.M.S.
can put your last
good nerve, to the test.

If a man could be a woman
and a woman could be a man
there could be perfect peace
for then we would all understand.

How one woman's
blessing in disguise
is another's monthly curse
For it is the very essence
of life, that brings forth every
child of the universe.

Mad at Mother Nature

Feelin' unloved, unwanted
overweight, bloated and fat
cuz you got the evil-gal blues
and feelin' ugly as a bat.

With an insatiable
cravin' for chocolate
like the taste of Baby Ruth
sometimes, you get so helplessly
horny, it's enough to give you
a sweet tooth.

Can't eat, can't sleep
emotional ups downs
you just can't explain
and at times, it hurts so good
you just can't stand the pain.

When Mother-Nature
puts Father Time on hold
the life blood, of all life
is in the delicate nature
of her life givin' soul.

And I can't help
but be caught up
in the body of the mind
cuz I'm blood-mad
at Mother-Nature
for foolin' Father Time.

CR 24/7 x 9

From the womb
To the tomb
Cr. 24/7 x 9
Is all that's on my mind.

The foundation of black self
Respect, is black self love
for the violence of racism
Is white-hand in black glove.

And it's not about hate
Or simply bein' unkind
But a codifield-consciousness
Is a counter racists state of mind.

The higher self is a lethal
Weapon of war, and self respect
For the nature of the white king
Is to keep the black king in check.

And now that push
Has finally come to shove
CR. twenty four, seven x nine
Equals black-self love.

White folk's number one
Priority-consideration
Is the fear of white genetic
Annihilation.

For the 'cause n' effect
Of racism, no longer
Will we forever be
A welcome mat for injustice
Or mere pawns on the chess
Board of white supremacy.

Our one and only
Priority mission, and will
Is to bring white world
Supremacy to stand still.

A sense of self
And the lack of choas
In a counter racist state
Can only make a blackman
The kind of person, white folk
Love to hate.

So from the womb
To the tomb
CR. twenty four, seven x nine
Is all that's on my mind.

Cuz all non-white
Victims of racism
Can only be free
When we demand justice
Thru the elimination
Of white supremacy.

And to decode the lies
We got to do, what we must
Cuz CR twenty four, seven x nine
Equals Just-Us.

Black Nation

Black Nation
Black Nation
We are at War
Say What you Want
Say What you Will
But SLEEP NO MORE ...

Wake-Up Call: the Final Call.
($11.95 + $2.00 postage and handling per book____)

Also Order Wings of the Whirlwind
($10.00 + $2.00 postage and handling per book____)

Name *(please print)* _____

Address _____

City _____

Please make checks payable to:
Queen's Palace Inc
PO Box 571
Bladensburg Md. 20701
301-927-0670